APR   2000

J
B
RIDE, S.

People to Know

Sally Ride

First American Woman in Space

Carole Ann Camp

Enslow Publishers, Inc.

44 Fadem Road	PO Box 38
Box 699	Aldershot
Springfield, NJ 07081	Hants GU12 6BP
USA	UK

Library of Congress Cataloging-in-Publication Data

Camp, Carole Ann.
    Sally Ride : first American woman in space / Carole Ann Camp.
        p.   cm. — (People to know)
    Includes bibliographical references and index.
    Summary: A biography of Sally Ride, who in 1983 became the first American
woman to travel in space.
    ISBN 0-89490-829-4
    1. Ride, Sally—Juvenile literature. 2. Women astronauts—United States—
Biography—Juvenile literature. [1. Ride, Sally. 2. Astronauts. 3. Women—
Biography.] I. Title. II. Series.
TL789.85.R5C36 1997
629.45'0092—dc21
    [B]   97-9339
                                                                              CIP
                                                                               AC

Printed in the United States of America

10 9 8 7 6 5 4

Illustration Credits: National Aeronautics and Space Administration
(NASA), pp. 4, 8, 14, 48, 52, 62, 71, 92, 95; Smithsonian Institution, pp. 20,
30, 37, 40, 55, 67, 74, 84.

Cover Illustration: Smithsonian Institution

Contents

Sally Ride

A Day in History

At 3:15 A.M. on June 18, 1983, Sally Ride wakes to the sound of her alarm clock. Today is the day for which she has trained for the past five years. At the astronaut crew quarters, Ride and her four fellow astronauts prepare for the launch. Cameras videotape every minute of their breakfast, their last earth meal for a week. In matching outfits of navy blue, they listen to last-minute instructions. The NASA nurse checks their blood pressure and pulse one more time. They put on their flight suits—blue pants and jackets displaying the Space Transportation System 7, or STS-7, insignia on the pocket.

A van takes the crew to the launchpad.

Silhouetted against the dark Florida morning sky, the space shuttle *Challenger* waits for liftoff and its second trip into space. The five-person crew—commander Robert Crippen, pilot Rick Hauck, and mission specialists Sally Ride, Norman Thagard, and John Fabian—climb onto the launchpad to the sounds of the spaceship's hissing and rumbling. The astronauts enter the elevator that takes them to a level close to the nose of the craft, 195 feet above the ground. Six technicians greet them as they enter the "white room," where they are dusted off. They crawl through a forty-inch-diameter hatchway into *Challenger*. They are strapped into their seats, Crippen and Hauck up front, Ride behind them in the middle, Fabian and Thagard in the rear.

All gear is checked and rechecked, especially the oxygen to their helmets. Radio communication with Mission Control is checked again and again. Procedure manuals and checklists are readily available. On this mission, Ride acts as flight engineer.

The last minutes of the yearlong wait slip away. The sound of the closing hatch tells the astronauts that they are now alone on the launchpad. The technicians and all the flight personnel move away to watch. Over half a million people have gathered for this history-making liftoff, including more than one thousand reporters and media staff. People who have worked hard to encourage equal rights for women, such as Gloria Steinem and Jane Fonda, are among the throngs invited to watch the liftoff. This is no ordinary launching for those in the crowd. This launching marks the first time in history that an American woman will fly in space. In fact, not only is Sally Ride the first American woman to orbit the earth in a spacecraft, but at thirty-two, she is also the youngest American ever to fly in space. Anticipation and expectations are running high.

Lying on their backs, with the nose of *Challenger* pointed toward heaven, the astronauts of the seventh mission in the shuttle series wait as the last minutes and seconds slowly tick away.

At seven minutes to launch, they hear the walkway pull away. The astronauts close their visors a final time and oxygen flows into their helmets. The craft shudders as the power units start. Another shudder as the three launch engines ignite. Three seconds to blastoff. The rockets ignite. The spacecraft soars into space in a rush of steam, leaving a trail of fire and the launching pad far below.

Inside the shuttle the astronauts barely hear Mission Control above the thunder of the rockets. The trip is rough, very rough. Later Ride wrote, "For an instant I wonder if everything is working right. But there's no more time to wonder, and no time to be scared."[1] The spaceship speeds through the clouds. Out past the earth's atmosphere, it continues to accelerate as it ascends into the inky blackness of space.

Two minutes into the flight, the crew members feel pushed against the backs of their seats with a force three times their normal weight. They can barely move. The sensation becomes unpleasant. Ride writes, "After a couple of minutes of 3 g's, we're uncomfortable, straining to hold our books on our

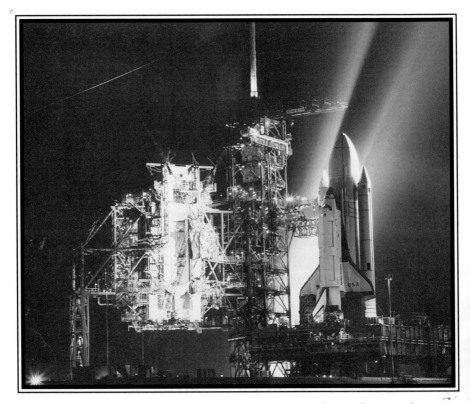

The space shuttle looks impressive against the nighttime sky. When dawn breaks, the shuttle will blast off, carrying the crew into the mysteries of space.

laps and craning our necks against the force to read the instruments. I find myself wishing we'd hurry up and get into orbit."[2]

The solid rocket boosters burn their fuel and drop into the ocean by parachute. The big empty fuel tank drops away to the earth. As the crew prepares to enter orbit, objects begin to float freely around the cabin. History is made: Sally Ride is in space.

From the ground at Mission Control, Ride's husband, Steven Hawley, a fellow astronaut scheduled to fly in a future mission, watches and listens. Once in space, Ride asks Mission Control, "Have you ever been to Disneyland? This was definitely an E ticket."[3] An E ticket was the ticket once used to get on the best rides at Disneyland.

At fifty miles above the surface of the earth, the space shuttle is officially in space, but it is not in orbit yet. The shuttle would fall back to earth if it did not enter an orbit. Additional pushes from smaller space engines get the shuttle into orbit about two hundred miles above the surface of the earth. Once in orbit, the spacecraft carrying Sally Ride and the rest of the *Challenger* crew will orbit the earth every ninety minutes traveling at a speed of five miles per second. The view of the earth from space is breathtaking. From the vantage point of *Challenger*'s orbit, Ride describes her experience:

> We still have a significant view. The sparkling blue oceans and bright orange deserts are glorious against the blackness of space. Even if we can't see the whole planet, we can see quite a distance. When

we are over Los Angeles we can see as far as Oregon; when we are over Florida we can see New York.[4]

Forty-four minutes and twenty-seven seconds after liftoff, *Challenger* reaches its final orbit, two hundred miles above the earth's surface. After twenty-two years, thirty-six "manned" missions, and fifty-seven astronauts, the United States has put a woman in space.

Growing Up

Sally Kristen Ride was born on
May 26, 1951, in Los Angeles, California, to Dale and
Joyce Ride. Dale Ride taught political science at
Santa Monica College. Sally Ride's mother, Joyce,
who was also a teacher, enjoyed reading and
encouraged her children to develop their own skills
and talents. When Sally and her younger sister,
Karen, were young, their mother stayed at home to
take care of them. She kept busy doing volunteer
work at Encino Presbyterian Church and counseling
at a nearby women's prison. She also taught English
to foreign students. Joyce and Dale Ride guided their
children gently through childhood in an uncritical
and respectful way. Ride's father said, "We just let

them [Sally and Karen] develop normally. We might have encouraged, but mostly we let them explore."[1] Sally and Karen, nicknamed "Bear" because Sally could not say "Karen" when she was little, lived in a home where there were many books and many visitors.

By the age of five Sally liked to read, especially the newspaper. She liked the sports pages best because they were filled with scores and the ratings of players, like batting averages, that she had fun memorizing. She had an incredible memory. She enjoyed reading mystery stories and science fiction, especially about her favorite sleuths, Nancy Drew and James Bond. Like other children of her age in the 1950s, young Sally held Superman among her favorite heroes.

Sally loved sports even more than reading. She played all kinds of street games, including baseball, football, and soccer, but her favorite was softball. The young boys in the neighborhood noticed her talents early. She was often the only girl allowed to play on the boys' teams. In fact, many times she was the first person picked when the boys chose their teams. Her early life experience taught her that it was all right for girls to compete in boys' games.

Joyce Ride tried to encourage Sally to take piano lessons, but learning to play the piano did not appeal to Sally. Her mother said, "The main thing was that if Sally was interested in a subject, she'd give it all her attention. If she wasn't interested, she didn't give it her attention. She sets her own goals."[2]

When Sally was nine, the family traveled in Europe for a year. During the trip Joyce and Dale Ride tutored their daughters. The year of travel provided the young Ride girls with many wonderful opportunities. Sally and Karen held many precious memories of the trip. They chose to hold on to their experience of that year by naming their pet collie in honor of the dog they had had while living in what was then the country of Yugoslavia.

Back home in Santa Monica, the family often entertained people who came from different countries and cultures. Both of these opportunities, world travel and foreign visitors, helped to broaden Sally's understanding of the world.

Although Sally was always a very good student in school, she passed her elementary and middle school years almost unnoticed. She had a very quiet, almost shy personality. Wilbur Hansen, one of her teachers at Portola Junior High School, remembers, "In my class, Sally was quiet, did her work, and was very private. . . . I wouldn't say she was remarkable in any way—she was just a good student."[3]

Sally's interest in sports eventually led her to play tennis. She loved practicing against the garage door. Hour after hour she would hit the ball, trying to aim at exactly the right spot. She challenged everyone and anyone who would play with her. When she was eleven, her enthusiasm and skill led to lessons from four-time women's national champion Alice Marble.

While still a teenager, Sally ranked nationally as an amateur. Her skill in tennis led to a scholarship to Westlake School for Girls, a small private high school in Los Angeles, California. The headmaster of the school played tennis with her on many occasions. In

At age nine Sally Ride traveled in Europe with her family for a year. She learned about many different nations and people. Ride would get an even broader perspective of the earth one day as an astronaut viewing our beautiful planet from far above.

one match he made the mistake of showing off after he had gotten a particularly good shot past her in a doubles match. He remembers, "She looked at me, smiled rather malevolently and then fired . . . three successive drives aimed right between the eyes."[4] However, Sally competed mostly with herself, spending many hours a day perfecting a particular shot. She never settled for second best.

One of Ride's science teachers, Elizabeth Mommaerts, introduced Ride to her second love. As a junior in high school, Ride was in Mommaerts's physiology class, learning about living things and how they work. This class was a turning point in Ride's life. She became really excited about science, the scientific method, and the scientific way of thinking and organizing information.

The scientific method for solving problems involves several steps: observation, hypothesizing, gathering data, organizing data, and drawing conclusions. Scientists use this method of experimentation, along with careful measurements and analysis of data, to gain a better understanding of the universe.

Ride discovered during this school year that she loved to solve problems. The scientific method appealed to her logical mind. Dr. Mommaerts was so impressed by Sally's scholastic abilities that she encouraged her to pursue a career in science. Mommaerts replaced Superman as Sally's role model. Later, describing her high school teacher, Ride said, "She was obviously intelligent, clear thinking and extremely logical. . . . I had never seen logic personified before."[5] These characteristics also describe Ride.

Ride and Mommaerts were friends until Mommaerts's death in 1972.

Ride was a good student, but her mother reflected, "If she was bored in the classroom . . . she would not make an effort. It irritated some teachers. One saw her as a clock-watcher. . . . The class was dull, and Sally was bored."[6]

Sally spent so much of her time practicing tennis that she did not participate in many of the school clubs, take part in school social groups, or attend parties. Her primary interest was to continue to improve her skills in tennis. She says that her parents did not push her in any particular direction "except to make sure I studied and brought home the right kind of grades."[7]

Growing up, Sally never questioned society's attitudes that women and men were suited for different kinds of work. She just assumed that she could do anything she wanted to. Her life so far had been a success: a success in sports and a success in school. She believed in herself. She went to college in 1969 looking forward to her future career as a scientist.

College Days

After graduating as one of the top six students from Westlake School for Girls in 1969, Ride went on to Swarthmore College in Swarthmore, Pennsylvania, where she intended to follow her love of science. She majored in physics and also continued to play tennis. Ride won the Eastern Intercollegiate Women's Tennis championship two years in a row. She wanted to become even more proficient in the sport, but unfortunately, her tennis playing in college was limited by the weather. Swarthmore did not have indoor courts at this time, so tennis was not a winter sport on the Pennsylvania campus. Ride longed for the warm weather of southern California where she could play tennis all year long. She began to get homesick. Finally she decided to leave Swarthmore. Ride returned to California, where she transferred to Stanford University in Palo Alto. She enrolled in math and science courses, still pursuing her goal of becoming a scientist. Her favorite courses were in the field of astronomy, especially astrophysics. Physics is the study of matter and energy and of the interaction between the two. Astrophysics is the branch of astronomy that deals with the physics of stars and other objects in space.

During her years as an undergraduate at Stanford University, Ride continued to be a very tough tennis competitor. Billie Jean King, a Wimbledon champion and one of America's greatest women tennis stars, noticed Ride's talent in tennis. King tried to persuade Ride to give up science and to pursue tennis as a career. Even though Ride's sister, Karen, believed that her sister was "a tough, no-nonsense competitor" who "will wipe you out every time,"[1] Sally reluctantly decided that she did not have what it took to become a tennis professional. Ride's father said, "She knows what she can do, and she likes to win."[2] When Ride gave up trying to become a tennis champion, her mother said, "She stopped playing tennis because she couldn't make the ball go just where she wanted it to. . . . It offended her that the ball wouldn't go just where she wanted."[3]

After two years of studying math and science, Ride discovered English literature and fell in love with Shakespeare. She said that she needed "a break from the equations."[4] Her approach to studying Shakespeare was different from most other students'. She saw Shakespeare's writing as a problem to be solved. In a unique way Shakespeare appealed to Ride's logical, problem-solving mind. She says, "I really had fun reading Shakespeare's plays and writing papers on them. . . . It's kind of like doing puzzles. You had to figure out what he was trying to say and find all the little clues inside the play [to prove] that you were right."[5]

Ride does not waste words in her speaking or in her writing. She quickly understands the solution to a problem and can explain it in a few words. According to one of her friends from college, Molly Tyson:

> She would turn in three pages, and that was it. But she would always see to the heart of things. . . . She used to drive English seminar teachers crazy. In a seminar you're dependent on discussion. Her style is to quickly think, figure it out, crystallize it. What she said was always very convincing, so there was no need to continue.[6]

She also does not volunteer information. Her sister said, "If you want to know something about Sally, you have to ask her."[7]

Ride's keen mind and incredible speed in solving problems made her an ideal candidate for her future as an astronaut. It also helped her in many everyday ways. One night, for example, while Ride and Molly Tyson were driving on a dark and deserted California road, their truck broke down. Ride, without even the mildest concern for their situation, hopped out of the truck and fixed the burst radiator hose with a roll of

Sally Ride spent her school years perfecting her tennis game and pursuing her goal of becoming a scientist. Her sharp mind and athletic abilities would make her an ideal candidate for an astronaut.

adhesive tape she found in the back. There was also a saucepan that Ride used to get water to fill the radiator. In less than an hour, Ride had solved the problem and the two were back on the road again. Tyson described her friend as "very resourceful." Tyson never saw Ride make a mistake. Ride was always cool, calm, and totally focused. Tyson said, "I've never seen Sally trip, on or off the court, physically or intellectually."[8]

Ride graduated from college in 1973 with bachelor's degrees in both English and physics. Very few students are able to fulfill the requirements for two degrees, especially in subjects that are so different. Her college days were not just all study, though. She also stayed in good physical shape by running five miles a day and playing intramural sports. She even played rugby.

After graduation, Ride continued her studies at Stanford University. She earned a master of science degree in physics in 1975. This was soon followed by a doctor of philosophy degree in astrophysics, conferred in 1978 by Stanford. One of Ride's colleagues in the physics department at Stanford, Jim Eckstein, said, "Everyone thought she was very good. But she was one of us. She quietly handled more than any of us here, and she never made a big deal about being a woman in the physics department."[9]

Although Ride is primarily known as an astronaut, she was also a pioneer in another field traditionally dominated by men: astrophysics. Ride did an in-depth study of the X rays that are given off by stars. Her work with lasers contributed to her acceptance into the astronaut program. Some thought that Ride's research might help develop ways to send energy back to the earth from space stations. She was just finishing work for her Ph.D. dissertation and serving as a research assistant in the physics department when she applied to become an astronaut.

Decision Day

Sally Ride's life story and career
are closely intertwined with the history and story of
the National Aeronautics and Space Administration
(NASA), which was founded in the late 1950s. In 1957
President Dwight D. Eisenhower established the
Scientific Advisory Committee, headed by Dr. James
R. Killian, president of the Massachusetts Institute of
Technology. The purpose of the committee was to
determine the goals of the United States and its future
in space. The committee suggested that it would
be better if one civilian organization had the
responsibility for overseeing an aggressive space
exploration program. This would include all the
scientific exploration, both manned and unmanned,

for the United States. The new organization would develop ways to cooperate with other nations in space-related activities, such as designing and operating satellites for communications and weather observations. The committee did not think that this new organization should be part of the Department of Defense. They did suggest, however, that any discoveries made through such an organization might benefit the military needs of the country. The Space Act, enacted by Congress on October 1, 1958, declared that "it is the policy of the United States that activities in space should be devoted to peaceful purposes for the benefit of all mankind."[1] In 1958, T. Keith Glennan, president of the Case Institute of Technology, became the first administrator of this new organization: the National Aeronautics and Space Administration, known by its popular name, NASA.

NASA, established only two days before the Soviet Union launched *Sputnik*, the first artificial earth satellite, set up three primary objectives:

> *(1) To conduct scientific exploration of space for the United States, (2) To begin exploration of space and the solar system . . . , (3) To apply space science and technology to the development of earth satellites for peaceful purposes to promote human welfare.*[2]

Less than three years later, on May 5, 1961, Alan Shepard became the first American to be launched into space. His flight in *Freedom 7* lasted fifteen minutes and thirty seconds and did not go into orbit. Nine months later, John Glenn, in *Friendship 7*, became the first American to orbit the earth.

Important events in NASA's history and in the history of space flight followed rapidly. However, the Soviet space program was progressing even faster. On April 12, 1961, a month before Shepard's flight, Yuri Gagarin was the first human to make an orbital flight. His flight in *Vostok 1* lasted one hour and forty-eight minutes. In August 1961, another Soviet astronaut circled the earth seventeen times, staying in space for twenty-five hours and eighteen minutes. In June 1963, twenty years and two days before Ride's historic flight, Soviet astronaut Valentina Tereshkova became the first woman in space. Her flight lasted seventy hours and fifty minutes.

In 1961, President John F. Kennedy challenged the United States to get to the moon before the Soviets. In his famous speech to Congress, he jump-started the space race with the Soviet Union:

> *Now is the time to take longer strides—time for a greater new American enterprise—time for this Nation to take a clearly leading role in space achievement which in many ways may hold the key to our future on earth. . . .*
>
> *Space is open to us now; and our eagerness to share its meaning is not governed by the efforts of others. We go into space because whatever mankind must undertake, free men must fully share. . . .*
>
> *I believe that this Nation should commit itself to achieving the goal, before this decade is out, of landing a man on the moon and returning him safely to earth.*[3]

Eight years later, in 1969, Neil Armstrong was the first human being to walk on the moon.

NASA first began designing the STS, or the Space Transportation System, in 1969. After receiving approval from Congress, NASA announced its space shuttle program. By 1972 the design was complete and Rockwell International contracted to build the vehicles.

One of the purposes of the STS program was to use the same spacecraft for many different missions. Until that time most of the spacecraft used in the Mercury, Gemini, and Apollo programs were not reusable for other flights. Reusing a spacecraft would save money in future building costs. In addition, the spacecraft NASA planned to use were large enough to deliver equipment and supplies back and forth to future space stations.

Another aspect of the program would be to have private industry pay NASA to launch satellites used for television and telephone communication. NASA was in the perfect position to carry these private-industry satellites, referred to as payloads, into orbit.

NASA engineers designed the cockpits of the crafts to hold larger crews. There were five spacecraft, or Orbiting Vehicles (OV), scheduled for the original STS fleet: *Challenger* (OV-099), *Discovery* (OV-103), *Atlantis* (OV-104), *Columbia* (OV-102), and *Enterprise* (OV-101). The *Enterprise* never flew on a mission. It was used only to test various aspects of the flight.

In 1978 major changes took place at NASA. Until that time NASA had been hiring people who were pilots by profession, primarily military pilots. NASA had not needed many new pilots for nearly ten years.

The development of the STS program meant that more people could be accommodated on board a spacecraft. Not every astronaut would have to be a pilot. NASA decided that scientists could be astronauts, too. With this vision of a greatly expanded program, NASA had to begin actively recruiting new astronauts. They specifically looked for young scientists who were excellent scholars and researchers in their fields—and who were also willing to put aside their own research and pursue space science for a few years.

Carolyn Huntoon, a member of the astronaut selection committee, commented:

> *Because we had a new spacecraft, and it was going to be built so that it had space inside it . . . and could have toilet facilities that could accommodate women . . . and, I think, because at that time in our country, people were feeling a little bit bad about the way they treated women . . . , they said, "It's a federal job and we're going to open it to all races, sexes, religious backgrounds and ages."*[4]

To accommodate shorter people, including some women, the shuttle seats slid back and forth, much as a car seat does. Optional grooming aids were added to the personal kits of the astronauts, and the shuttle's bathroom was redesigned for use by both sexes.

NASA's new policy of recruiting women met with some resistance from the old-timers. Alan Bean, for example, an Apollo and Skylab veteran, was not pleased at first that women were being considered for the program. Later, however, he admitted, "At first I imagined they were just individuals trying to do a man's job. I was proven wrong. . . . Females intuitively understand astronaut skills. They perform the mental and physical tasks as well as men."[5]

In an attempt to attract young scientists, NASA advertised for astronauts in many college newspapers around the country. More than one thousand women and nearly seven thousand men responded to the ad and applied for the thirty-five slots open in the astronaut class of 1978.

Sally Ride was one of the young women to apply. At the time she was twenty-six years old and an astrophysicist working on her Ph.D. degree at Stanford University. She saw the job advertised in the *Stanford Daily*, the campus newspaper. The timing was right. Although she had always had an interest in space and astronomy, the goal of becoming an astronaut had not really occurred to her until she saw the ad. Then, almost in a flash, she knew that becoming an astronaut was something she really wanted to do. Ride said:

> *I was interested in space but it wasn't anything I built a career around. Instead I planned to go into research in physics. I wouldn't have known how to prepare for a career as an astronaut even if it had occurred to me to try, since women weren't involved in the space program at that time.*[6]

She immediately answered the ad. She said later, "I don't know why I wanted to do it," but she knew she could do it.[7] All of her life Ride's parents had taught her that she could do anything she wanted to do.

NASA sorted through the eight thousand applications and selected 208 finalists, including Sally

Ride. The finalists participated in an extensive interview process. They were interviewed several times by various committees as well as two psychiatrists. "We saw two psychiatrists for about forty-five minutes each," Ride said. "One of them was generally exactly what I had always pictured from a psychiatrist—[a person] who showed you the comfortable chair . . . and then asked you how you felt about your sister. Then the other . . . was sort of the bad guy psychiatrist, who tried to rattle you."[8] In another interview the candidates were asked many questions about their background, education, hobbies, research, and politics.

They also took physical and mental stress tests. One of the stress tests included being put into a small round compartment made of fabric, called the "crystal rescue sphere." In the compartment there was space for one person to be seated. It was designed so that an astronaut could transport a fellow crew member from one space vehicle to another if there were not enough pressurized space suits available for each person. The stress tests examined the candidates' reactions to stressful situations. Being an astronaut requires long, hard hours of tedious mental and physical work. The tests screened out people who thought that being an astronaut was just an exciting and glamorous job.

After the interview process, thirty-five people were selected as astronaut-candidates—fifteen space shuttle pilots and twenty mission specialists. Six of the mission specialists were women. Besides astrophysicist Sally Kristen Ride, the first class of women included Anna Fisher, medical doctor; Shannon Lucid, chemist; Margaret Seddon, surgeon;

Kathryn Sullivan, geologist; and Judith Resnik, electrical engineer.

Sally Ride had an extensive science background, and she was an athlete in excellent physical condition. She had good eyesight, and she was the right age. But most important, she was a team player, a skill learned when she was a child playing softball in the street with the boys in the neighborhood. All these qualities made her especially suited to the new astronaut program.

About eight thousand men and women applied to NASA's astronaut training program, but only thirty-five were selected as astronaut-candidates. Pictured here are Ride and a few fellow trainees.

On January 16, 1978, she received the long-anticipated telephone call from NASA. George Abbey said on the other end of the line, "Well, we've got a job here for you if you are still interested in taking it." Ride responded immediately: "Yes, sir!"[9]

When Ride hung up, she called her mother. Ride's mother later talked about that phone call: "Sally is normally very cool, very low key, but when she called to tell me the news, she was bordering on breathless."[10] Ride's family had always encouraged the two daughters to follow their own paths, but Ride commented, "I think my Dad was kind of happy when I became an astronaut. . . . Before I joined NASA I was in theoretical astrophysics. Astronaut was a concept he understood."[11]

At first, Ride claims, she never thought she would get into the final group of people selected to be astronauts. She thought that she was going to work as a physicist when she graduated from college. She said, "I don't know why I wanted to do it. I never had any burning ambition to be in the space program. . . . I never even thought about how they recruited astronauts. When I saw them on TV, they all seemed to be Navy or Air Force test pilots. I suppose I just took it for granted that it was pretty much a closed club."[12]

Ride moved to Johnson Space Center in Houston, Texas, the control center for NASA spacecraft missions, in 1978.

All the Right Stuff

In July 1978, Ride reported to NASA's Johnson Space Center just outside Houston, Texas. More than seventeen thousand people worked at the center, which looked like a college campus. For Ride and the astronaut class of 1978, it was back to school. They had been recruited for the Space Transportation System program (STS). Ride and her fellow classmates were expected to learn all about STS. In addition to taking classes on the basic shuttle systems, each also had to become an expert on one aspect of the shuttle. During the first year, Ride and the other trainees studied the shuttle. They also took courses in mathematics, meteorology, astronomy, navigation, physics, and computers.

Most of their time was spent learning about the shuttle orbiter. New astronaut-candidates spent eight-hour days at the Shuttle Avionics Integration Laboratory, SAIL, a noisy place where machinery hummed all day and all night. Here astronaut-candidates worked with the SAIL workers, learning about every wire and circuit on the shuttle. Ride learned what to do if an emergency occurred or if a crew member got sick. She would have to be ready to take over.

There are three main parts to the space shuttle: the solid rocket boosters (SRBs), the orbiter, and the external tank. The tank, which is the largest part of the shuttle, holds the fuel burned during launch by the orbiter's three main engines. The solid rocket boosters provide the extra power needed for launch. An orbiter looks like a stubby, short-winged airplane, something like a DC-9 jet. When an orbiter reenters the earth's atmosphere after being out in space, the friction of the shuttle through air at such a high speed causes the shuttle to heat up. To keep the shuttle from burning up entirely during reentry, it is covered with insulation. This consists of about twenty-three thousand ceramic-coated silica fiber tiles on the underside of the shuttle, where the buildup of heat is the greatest.

The orbiter is the part of the shuttle that holds the astronauts and the cargo. Up to eight people can fit in the orbiter. In the upper level the astronauts operate the shuttle launchings and landings. Most of the other work, as well as sleeping and eating, takes place in the mid-deck compartment. This is also where many of the other experiments of each flight are carried out. The mid-deck compartment has an airlock that opens into the payload (cargo) bay and allows access to space. All the other operating equipment—for example, the water pumps and the air purification systems—is located below the mid-deck floor. The life-support systems allow a shuttle to remain in orbit for up to thirty days.

Besides studying the technical aspects of the shuttle, Ride and the other trainees also had to prepare their bodies for the flight. Astronauts have to be in excellent physical condition so their bodies can withstand the rigors of training. NASA allowed the astronauts to plan their own exercise programs. Ride chose to run. She ran four miles a day during the week and eight to ten miles on weekends. She also continued to play tennis and volleyball. All astronauts must be able to carry the forty-five-pound parachute used in NASA's T-38 training jets. Ride added weight lifting to her workout program so that she would be strong enough.

Part of the training included hanging from a parachute for extended periods of time and being ejected out of a T-38 jet trainer. In another exercise, Ride, wearing a parachute, was dropped from a moving boat. She had to learn how to release the parachute while the boat dragged her along. Training was not always that thrilling. Sometimes Ride had to sit through long, boring meetings. "People think we're tossed into centrifuges, dunked into water, and thrown out of planes in this work . . . but it's not always exciting. We sit behind desks and go to meetings mostly."[1]

Although the shuttle scientists and other passengers no longer needed to be pilots, every crew member did have to know how the shuttle worked in case of an emergency. Each astronaut-candidate spent fifteen hours a month in the T-38, NASA's training jet. Ride enjoyed the flight training in the two-seat T-38 trainers so much that she chose to get her pilot's license. Ride became a proficient jet pilot and flight engineer. She would be capable of flying *Challenger* if she had to in an emergency.

Ride also trained in shuttle simulators that are run by computers. The simulators helped Ride learn what an actual flight feels like without leaving the ground. There are many types of simulators: the shuttle training aircraft simulator, the navigation simulator, the systems engineer simulator, the shuttle mission simulator, and the motion base simulator. Each simulator has a computer or mechanical device that duplicates the feel and response of a piece of equipment. While astronaut teams practiced a simulated shuttle flight together in a flight simulator, ground control teams also practiced their part of the operation. In April 1982, when Ride went into training for her first real flight, she spent twelve to fifteen hours a week in the shuttle simulator. She said, "We have a simulator in Houston that's very good . . . they turn you on your back and shake you and vibrate you and pump noise in, so that it's very realistic."[2]

Most of the experiences the astronauts would have while in space could be simulated fairly accurately on earth—except for the sensation of weightlessness.

As part of her astronaut training, Sally Ride had to hang from a parachute for long periods of time. All astronauts must be strong enough to carry a forty-five-pound parachute, so Ride added weight lifting to her workout routine.

Trying to simulate the sensation of weightlessness on earth is difficult. There are no places on earth where one is free from the earth's force of gravity. Gravity is the force that causes all objects with mass to attract each other.

One way Ride experienced the sensation of weightlessness for a brief time, usually not more than thirty seconds, was in NASA's KC-135 transport plane. The inside of the transport plane is empty, and the walls are padded. When the plane flies in a special high-speed curved path, called a parabola, the passengers experience a sense of weightlessness for a short time. It is like being in a free-fall ride at an amusement park or going down a steep roller-coaster drop.

During the half minute the astronauts float weight-lessly inside the jet, they practice different activities. After many flights, they have tried eating, drinking, putting on space suits, and using shuttle equipment in near weightlessness. Many astronauts become nauseated during these stomach-churning flights and have nicknamed the KC-135 the "vomit comet."

In addition to practice rides on the vomit comet, Ride spent many hours maneuvering in a space suit while underwater in a swimming pool. Being underwater is somewhat like being in the apparent weightlessness of space, although up and down are still clear underwater. Inside the shuttle on a real mission, there is no up or down.

Ride had many "firsts" in the space program. She was the first woman from the United States to fly into space, and the youngest American ever to fly in space. She and Steven Hawley were also the first two astronauts to marry each other. In July 1982 Ride and Hawley—a tall red-haired astronomer—had a small, informal wedding at Hawley's parents' home in Salina, Kansas. Only the immediate families were present. Ride flew a jet plane from Houston to Kansas for the occasion. She wore blue jeans and a rugby shirt. Two ministers performed the ceremony: the Reverend Dr. Bernard Hawley, Steven Hawley's father, and the Reverend Karen Scott, Sally Ride's sister. At the time of the wedding, Ride stated that she and Hawley did not plan to have children.

After a year of general training on the specifics of the shuttle itself, astronaut-candidate Ride graduated. As astronaut Ride, she became eligible for flight. First each astronaut spends at least two years and often as many as five years preparing for his or her unique assignment. Ride was assigned to study the Remote Manipulator System (RMS), a mechanical arm that moves objects in and out of the payload bay. Her job was to become an expert on the RMS. "I spent two years on it, and nothing else," Ride declared. "As far as I knew there was nothing else; what you did was launch an arm."[3]

John Fabian, another mission specialist, also practiced with the RMS, the fifty-foot robot arm that would be used to release and pick up satellites. Fabian and Ride went to Toronto to study and test the giant arm. They worked closely with the Canadian engineers to improve the design of the arm until its operation was virtually perfect. The astronauts had to be able to manipulate the arm instinctively.

The RMS was scheduled to be used on STS-7. As

Sally Ride especially liked flying. Each astronaut-candidate spent fifteen hours a month in the T-38, NASA's training jet. They needed to learn how to pilot the shuttle in case of an emergency.

mission specialists, Ride and Fabian also had to know about all the other experiments that would be aboard their mission. They studied every detail of each experiment that would be performed on the STS-7 flight. They also learned how the satellites that were to be launched during their mission worked.

The Space Transportation System flights began in 1977 with test flights of *Enterprise*, which was used to test the landing capabilities of the shuttle. *Enterprise* was taken to an altitude of twenty-two thousand feet by a Boeing 747 jet and released. It was then piloted back to Edwards Air Force Base. It was crucial to the success of the program that the shuttles be able to land safely. After many successful landings, NASA was ready to send astronauts into space and bring them home to earth again. This time the landing would be on an airstrip in California rather than in the Pacific Ocean. On April 12, 1981, John Young and Robert Crippen marked the beginning of the United States shuttle program by flying in *Columbia* (STS-1) for fifty-four hours and twenty-one minutes. They orbited the earth thirty-six times.

Even though only two astronauts were aboard this mission, many of the other astronauts were involved in activities related to the mission. Astronauts participated in one another's flights in a variety of ways. NASA believed that having astronauts experience all phases of a mission better prepared them for their own flight. During Young and Crippen's flight of STS-1, Ride rode in the back of a T-38 chase plane. The T-38 chase plane followed the shuttle from the upper atmosphere down to the landing strip. Astronauts in the plane took pictures and supplied wind and weather information to the crew of *Columbia.*

One of the most important ground jobs is that of capsule communicator, or capcom. The capcom is the only person at Mission Control who is allowed to talk to the astronauts in space. All communication from the ground to the spacecraft goes through the capcom. The capcom passes the advice of the scientists working in Houston to the astronauts in the spacecraft. This is so the astronauts in space can focus on just one voice, instead of trying to listen to a variety of voices and directions.

Astronauts serve as capcom. This helps the astronauts of future missions understand what is happening on the ground while they are in space. Ride served as capcom for *Columbia* missions STS-2 and STS-3. She was the first woman ever to do this important communications task.

Columbia flew several other missions before *Challenger* was launched. On November 11, 1982, *Columbia* mission STS-5, with astronauts Vance Brand, Robert Overmyer, Joseph Allen, and William Lenoir, lasted one hundred twenty-two hours. It was the first flight of a space shuttle to launch two commercial communication satellites.

Five months later NASA launched the first flight of the *Challenger* shuttle STS-6. Paul Weitz, Karol Bobko, Donald Peterson, and Franklin Musgrave were aboard. STS-6 carried one of the largest payloads ever into space. The payload weighed 46,615 pounds. Part of the payload was a tracking and data satellite designed to pick up radio waves from satellites and relay them to a station in White Sands, New Mexico. The astronauts sent the satellite into a geosynchronous orbit. This is an orbit around the earth at an altitude about 22,300 miles above the surface of the earth. When a satellite is at this altitude, it orbits the earth in the same amount of time that the earth turns. This means the satellite stays in the same place above the earth all the time. Astronauts on this flight also took the first space walk from a shuttle. They practiced repair techniques in the payload bay— which is behind the crew compartment and in front of the engines.

Two months after STS-6, NASA prepared to launch STS-7. The crew of the *Challenger* space shuttle's seventh flight included Sally Ride, along with Robert Crippen, Frederick Hauck, and John Fabian. There was also a physician on board. One phenomenon that had plagued NASA for years was the fact that many astronauts became space sick during the first part of the flight. NASA added Dr. Norman Thagard to the crew of STS-7 to study space sickness. This increased the number of crew members on STS-7 to five—the largest crew that NASA had ever launched into orbit.

On June 18, 1983, the United States launched *Challenger* space shuttle STS-7, carrying the first woman from the United States into space.

Life on the Inside

The day finally arrived. After five years of training, Sally Ride made history aboard *Challenger* flight STS-7. Thousands of people gathered for the liftoff. Reporters from newspapers and television stations around the world crowded the beaches of Cape Canaveral to witness this historic trip. Women active in the feminist movement were among those who had eagerly assembled in the early hours of the Florida morning. Jane Fonda, an actress and outspoken supporter of women's rights, said, "If I were in my teens and I read about her, I would certainly consider science or engineering, which I never would have before."[1] Gloria Steinem, one of the founders of the women's movement and the creator of

Ms. magazine, believed that this historic mission of STS-7 would significantly affect all future generations. She said, "It's an important first, because it means millions and millions of little girls are going to sit in front of the television and know they can become astronauts after this."[2]

Ride, however, did not see this event as anything special for women. Plagued by thousands of requests for interviews, Ride continually downplayed the historic significance of her first trip into space. She claimed, "I'm not historical material."[3] Later, in another interview, Ride said, "I did not come to NASA to make history. . . . It's important to me that people don't think I was picked for the flight because I am a woman and it's time for NASA to send one."[4] But the world had a different view. In spite of Ride's protests that she was nobody special and that she was just another astronaut doing her job, everyone was watching to see how well she did. Her reactions and her performance could seriously affect the future of other women trained to be astronauts. Television sets all over the country were tuned in to NASA's broadcast of this historic moment.

Inside *Challenger,* Ride and the crew of STS-7 waited eagerly for the mighty roar of the spacecraft's engines. Looking like characters from a *Peanuts* cartoon, the five astronauts in their "Snoopy Hats"—the last remains of the old space suits of science fiction movies—listened for instructions from ground control. To help the astronauts withstand the speed of liftoff, they were strapped into their seats lying on their backs with their feet slightly above their heads.

Pilot Hauck and Commander Crippen sat in the forward section of the spacecraft, which looked very much like the cockpit of a DC-9 jet plane. In every direction Hauck and Crippen looked, they saw control panels, above and below the windows, even above them on the ceiling. The panels consist of thousands of switches. There were no buttons, however, because buttons could easily be bumped into once the crew began to float around the cabin. Each operation was controlled by three separate switches. The second and third switches acted as backup.

Ride, seated behind the pilot, served as flight engineer. She monitored the blinking lights and flashing numbers, calling them off to the pilot and commander. Thagard and Fabian were strapped in behind.

The engines ignited. The spacecraft roared and shuddered. After a burst of flame and a cloud of steam, the voice of Mission Control told the world, "We have liftoff." Thousands of pairs of eyes followed the streak of the four-million-pound aluminum and ceramic flying machine as it passed out of sight. Inside the spacecraft, Ride was busy watching the dials and calling out data to the crew. Her training in the flight simulator had prepared her well for this moment.

About two minutes into the flight, the crew felt the force of three g's. It lasted a few minutes, and then the sensation eased. The great acceleration of the rocket was pushing their bodies forward at a rapidly increasing speed.

One "g" is the amount of force acting on a body by the force of gravity from the earth. In the earlier flights of Mercury and Apollo, the astronauts had experienced

In the space shuttle Challenger, *Sally Ride served as flight engineer. She monitored the blinking lights and flashing numbers, calling them off to the pilot and commander.*

a force of 8.1 g's. That meant that the force pushing them into their seats was 8.1 times what they normally felt on earth. In *Challenger* this force reached only about 3 g's. That is about what you might feel going around a corner in a car at a very high speed. *Challenger* was designed to reach orbit at a more gradual rate than the older spacecraft. So shuttle astronauts experienced a force closer to three times their normal weight.

The force of 3 g's lasted only two minutes, until the solid-fuel rocket boosters finished burning their fuel. The boosters were then dropped into the ocean by parachutes. The main engines continued burning liquid hydrogen and liquid oxygen. Six and a half minutes later, the big fuel tank dropped off. The shuttle then continued accelerating with the orbital maneuvering engines. It arrived at its orbiting position beyond the earth's atmosphere about forty-four minutes after liftoff. The voice of Mission Control told the world, "Space Shuttle Challenger has delivered to space the largest human payload of all time, four men and one woman."[5]

Once they were in space, the astronauts went right to work. On board were four satellites: two communications satellites and two satellites that were to return to earth with the shuttle after tests and experiments were conducted. Also on board were several "getaway specials"—experiments suggested by college and high school students, private companies, and government agencies. The astronauts began their workday by stowing the equipment that is used only for launching and landing. It would not be needed again for six days. Within two hours of launch the crew began sending television pictures back to Houston.

Being an astronaut requires a great deal of hard work. All the training of the past years had prepared the *Challenger* astronauts for the tasks that they were to accomplish in space. Mission specialists Ride and Fabian were ready for their first task: launching a satellite. They started the satellites spinning. This prelaunch spinning prevents satellites from wobbling in space after they are ejected. Fabian and Ride sent the satellite *Anik* (which means brother in the Inuit language) to an orbit about 22,300 miles above the earth's surface. This satellite is one of Canada's television communications satellites. Canada paid several million dollars to send *Anik* on this flight.

In addition to launching satellites, Ride had to learn how to move her body in this new environment, away from the earth's gravity. Ride said, "The best part of being in space is being weightless."[6] The feeling of weightlessness takes a while to get used to, but it is clear that Ride and other astronauts find many ways to enjoy the freedom of movement. Recently, scientists at NASA have replaced the term *zero gravity* with *microgravity*. The term microgravity is being used now because *zero gravity* implies no gravity. Objects on the surface of the earth are said to be acted upon by one g, or one earth gravity. In the microgravity environment of space, the weight of objects appears to be very, very small compared to their weight on the earth's surface.[7]

Throughout this flight and all other flights, doctors like Dr. Thagard performed extensive tests on the effects of space travel on human beings. In later flights, astronauts who were susceptible to space sickness wore a medicated adhesive strip behind one ear. Medicine slowly seeped through the skin to help prevent nausea.

Once astronauts adapt to microgravity, they often get playful, trying things that cannot be done on earth or would seem odd on earth. *Challenger* STS-7 astronauts floated jelly beans across the cabin for other crew members to catch in their mouths. The candy was donated to flight STS-7 by President Reagan, who was known for liking jelly beans.

Astronauts look a little different in space than they do on earth. On earth, body fluids like blood are pulled by gravity toward the feet. In space, however, body fluids are more evenly distributed around the body, causing the astronauts to have puffy faces. In addition, most astronauts get taller in space by about an inch. This is because gravity is not pulling the body toward the floor, as on earth. In space the spinal column can stretch out, and astronauts become a bit taller. NASA engineers designed the astronauts' clothes so they will fit during space flight. Elasticized thread is used so the clothes can adjust to shrinking waistlines, thinning legs, and lengthening bodies.

Ride and other crew members in space for their first mission had to learn how to move around. It was not the same as moving in water, as they had practiced in the pool on earth. In water you can push against the water to move, but in a spacecraft, air is the only thing to push against, and it is not dense enough to allow the astronauts to "swim" around. Ride soon learned that she had to push against a surface to start moving. Unfortunately, she pushed too hard at first and crashed into the opposite wall. Once she pushed off from a surface, there was no slowing down until she hit something. Gradually, Ride learned how much to push to move safely from one place to another. "Early in my first flight," she said, "I constantly felt that I was about to lose control, as though I were teetering on a balance beam or tipping over in a canoe. It's a strange, unsteady feeling that's difficult to describe, but fortunately it goes away."[8]

In a rush of steam and thunder of rockets, the shuttle soars into space. "For an instant I wonder if everything is working right. But there's no more time to wonder, and no time to be scared," wrote Sally Ride about her first flight in the Challenger.

When they are first learning how to move, astronauts often try to go feetfirst down the ladder and headfirst up the ladder. When the shuttle is in space, there is no real down or up. Astronauts soon learn that headfirst works best regardless of where they are trying to go.

Besides learning how much push was needed to get from one place to another, Ride also had to learn how to stay in one place. Even the tiniest push made her drift slowly across the cabin. This was also true for all the equipment in the spacecraft. Everything had to be anchored down. Ride said, "After a day or two I got the knack of staying still and could change clothes without tumbling backwards."[9]

On *Challenger*, everyone took a turn preparing the meals. In the early days of human space flight, many experiments were carried out to find easy and nutritious ways to eat in microgravity. John Glenn, the first United States astronaut to circle the earth, was one of the experimenters. Some people had feared that the most difficult part about eating in space would be swallowing. It turned out that swallowing was easy. The bigger problem was getting the food into the mouth. Liquids and crumbs were a particular nuisance. The crumbs floated around the cabin, getting into equipment. Later, food was designed with a gummy gelatin coating that helped it stick to utensils and packaging.

Some of the food on *Challenger* was dehydrated or freeze-dried, but other food was fresh. Hot dogs, for example, were packed in foil ready to eat. Meats and most other foods had to be thermostabilized. This is a process of heating food to kill bacteria and prevent spoilage. Breads and other bakery products were treated with radiation to keep them fresh. Nuts, granola bars, and candy did not need treatment.

The galley, or kitchen, of *Challenger* resembled a vending machine, except the astronauts did not have to put money in the slot to get the food out. The food that had been prepared and packaged on earth was designed to be nutritious and healthy. It was also meant to taste good. Each meal was labeled according to day and time. Some parts of the meal needed to be heated in the oven, like the hot dogs. Other foods needed to have water squirted into the packages. All liquids were in closed containers with straws, somewhat like juice boxes. The opening around the straw was tight to prevent the liquid from floating free. If some liquid did escape from its container it formed into the shape of a ball. In space, because there is no up or down, astronauts could just as easily have lunch on the "ceiling" as on the "floor."

Over the years, NASA discovered that astronauts had stuffy noses while floating in apparent weightlessness. Because smell is so connected with taste, this nasal congestion had caused earlier astronauts to complain that the food did not have any flavor. At the astronauts' suggestions, NASA spiced up the menu offerings.

Challenger circled the earth every ninety minutes. The astronauts could watch sixteen sunrises and sixteen sunsets every twenty-four hours. Sleep had to be scheduled according to the clock, not according to the sun, so the astronauts could get a good night's rest.

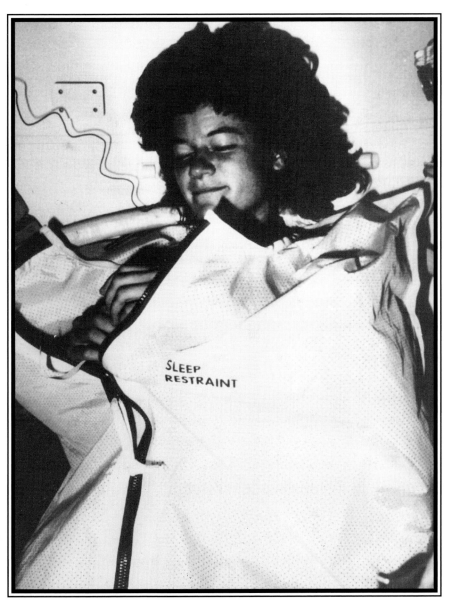

Sally Ride sleeps in the Challenger. *Without this sleep restraint she would float weightlessly around the cabin.*

One astronaut stayed up on watch while the others slept in the bunkroom, which was in an alcove across from the galley. The bunkroom contained four bunks, but because there was no floor or ceiling or top or bottom, two of the bunks were back to back, like two sides of a coin, with a board between them. A third bunk was arranged at a right-angle to the two-sided bunk. The bunk was a padded board with a fireproof sleeping bag. The padded board was designed to give the illusion of a comfortable mattress. However, an astronaut did not actually lie down on it. The purpose of the sleeping bag was to keep the sleeping astronauts gently strapped to the wall, floor, or ceiling, so they would not float around and bump into walls, people, or equipment. A sleeping astronaut's body relaxes into a natural state. The arms float out in front of the body at shoulder height. Many astronauts prefer to tuck their arms into the sleeping bag rather than have them float free.

At the end of the first day, Ride drifted into her sleeping space. Above her was a small light for reading, just like at home. But instead of watching television before she closed her eyes, she watched the earth far outside the window. Listening to music, she watched as the countries she visited as a child slid past. She realized that there were no boundaries on earth, no lines drawn on the surface of the planet to separate people from one another. She closed her eyes and fell asleep.

Mission Specialist

Ride opened her eyes on the second day to early-morning music and Father's Day greetings from Mission Control. Ride's fellow astronauts had ten children among them. For Ride, the day began much as it did on earth, except in a very small space and without any sense of gravity. NASA provided some privacy for the astronauts as they performed their morning routines. A privacy curtain had been added to the shuttle's design to create a bathroom area. Next to the galley was a personal hygiene station with a light and a mirror. To wash her hands, Ride first put her hands through flexible cuffs and then into a spray chamber. A jet stream of water poured into the chamber. Then the water was sucked out into a disposal tank so it would not escape into the cabin. If water got into the cabin, it could float around causing problems with the equipment. The astronauts never worried about using too much water because water was produced on board: *Challenger* generated its own electricity by fuel cells that combined liquid hydrogen and liquid oxygen. Pure water was the by-product of producing electricity in this way.

All the astronauts had personal hygiene kits with typical items for getting ready in the morning: toothpaste and toothbrush, dental floss, washcloths and towels, soap, deodorant, comb, brush, lip balm, and skin lotions. Ride's male companions also had a tube of shaving cream and a razor. The washcloths had been coated with a special chemical that cleaned without being wet.

Ride wrote in her book *To Space and Back* that the question she was most often asked was how astronauts go to the bathroom. In some ways *Challenger*'s bathroom was like any bathroom on earth. It even had a reading light. Of course, most bathrooms on earth do not have such an amazing view—the whole earth floating beyond the window. The shuttle's bathroom had been designed with women in mind. Instead of the flexible hose used by the all-male crews of the earlier Gemini and Apollo spacecraft, NASA provided a wide cuplike attachment that fit snugly between the legs to collect urine. To use the toilet Ride had to put her feet into toeholds and fasten the seat belt that was provided. The toilet seat belt and foot restraints kept Ride from floating off the seat.

Another major difference between earth toilets and

space toilets is in how the waste products are collected. The space toilet has a control panel. To the right of the seat is a handle. Pushing the handle forward opens the gate valve. A fan pulls air through the toilet and carries any wastes into a tank below. In the tank the solid waste is shredded into thin layers which are treated with chemicals. These layers dry quickly and are then sucked into a holding tank. Urine is held in another tank and dumped overboard from time to time. It soon vaporizes in the vacuum of space.

After breakfast on day two, the *Challenger* crew got ready to launch a second satellite, called *Palapa B*. This satellite was to be the communications link for all the islands of Indonesia.

In addition to launching satellites, Ride and Fabian were also responsible for all the other experiments that were on board. One of the original ideas behind the shuttle missions was that the shuttle would carry experiments into space for experimenters who were not part of NASA but would pay for the service. These getaway specials (experiments that "get away" from earth's gravity) cost the experimenters between $3,000 and $10,000. On this mission, Ride and Fabian were responsible for seven getaway specials. Some of these experiments were designed by high school students, some by college students, and many by people in industry.

One of the experiments was designed to observe the behavior of ants in microgravity. Television cameras monitored the ant colony throughout the flight. Some inner-city high school students from Camden,

New Jersey, had sent the ant colony. Students from California Technical Institute had sent an experiment that involved growing radishes from seed. The experimenters wanted to see where the radish seeds sent their roots when there was no up or down. Students from what was West Germany in 1983 also wanted to experiment with plant growth in outer space.

Crystal growing in microgravity was of special interest to many manufacturers on earth. Ride carefully monitored crystal growth experiments. Crystals grown in space are more perfectly formed, and scientists can analyze them better. She also performed experiments that tested technologies for making glass and different metal alloys related to glassmaking. Microgravity provides unique laboratory conditions not possible on earth. Many other experiments aboard this mission and later missions helped in the development of medical tasks like blood-flow measurements and the manufacture of pharmaceuticals. Conducting and monitoring all these experiments was the main daily task of mission specialists like Sally Ride.

One observer of many NASA flights said that the tone of conversation on STS-7 was more playful and bantering than the NASA jargon heard on earlier missions. The observer attributed this change to Ride, who had a reputation for comic one-liners. Mission Control in Houston heard Ride say, "[There are] three turkeys and two hams aboard," but Houston never knew who she thought were the hams and who the turkeys.[1] When Fabian said good night to his wife, he used the closing line from the famous American comedian Jimmy Durante's routine: "Good night, Mrs. Calabash, wherever you are." Ride then ended the broadcast with "Who was that masked man?"—a line from the television series *The Lone Ranger*.[2] By the end of the third day the humor and kidding around were well under way. The crew ended the day's communication with Houston by doing the closing routine from the television series *The Waltons*, each one saying good night to the others, name by name. The last good-night was to Houston, "Good night, John Boy."[3]

For two years Ride and Fabian had practiced day in and day out, learning how to maneuver the long robot arm. One of the reasons Ride was selected for this particular flight was that she was an expert in the manipulation of the robot arm and this was the flight where the robot arm was to be tested. On Ride's fifth day on the flight of STS-7, the time finally arrived. The fifty-foot-long pole, about the diameter of a telephone pole, with its four joints that can be twisted, turned, and folded into a variety of configurations, was about to take center stage. Imagine your own arm with extra elbows! One of Ride's tasks for this day was to test the flexibility and reliability of this fancy arm, which became affectionately known as the cherry picker.

As *Challenger* orbited the earth about 181 miles above the surface, Ride gave commands to Fabian, who pushed the buttons on the console. Looking out into the cargo bay, Ride watched as she guided the great mechanical arm slowly toward the Shuttle Pallet Satellite, or SPAS. The SPAS weighed about thirty-three

Sally Ride was known for her great sense of humor. Here, she shares a laugh with fellow mission specialist John Fabian during a preflight crew mission test.

hundred pounds on earth and was a self-contained laboratory built in what was then West Germany. One newspaper described the SPAS as a twenty-three-million-dollar flying bedstead.[4] It carried a television camera and eight experiments. One of the experiments measured the effect the shuttle had on its immediate environment. The SPAS was also designed to provide a laboratory for experiments that were sensitive to even the slightest vibration. Just the movement of the astronauts around the cabin of the shuttle was enough to cause *Challenger* to vibrate. These vibrations would not be felt in the SPAS when the SPAS was in orbit by itself separate from the shuttle.

Very carefully and very slowly, Ride lifted the SPAS from the cargo bay, released it, then quickly recaptured it. It was important not to lose the SPAS. Part of the experiment included monitoring what effect *Challenger*'s movements had on the SPAS. Ride released the SPAS again, and Crippen fired a small maneuvering engine to move *Challenger* about one thousand feet ahead of the SPAS. The exhaust from *Challenger* caused the SPAS to spin much faster than the scientists at Houston had anticipated. The influence of the shuttle exhaust on the satellite was an important discovery for future NASA operations, especially those where astronauts would make space walks to repair disabled satellites.

If Ride and the crew were successful in deploying and retrieving this satellite, then other NASA missions could begin to retrieve satellites that had malfunctioned. They could either bring them back to earth for repair or fix them in space and set them in their orbit again. Over the course of the day, Ride released and retrieved the satellite several times. Dr. Thagard, who served as backup, was given a turn. Fortunately, the procedure in which the satellite was released and retrieved proved successful.

Ride noticed that when the satellite was away from *Challenger*, the temperature in the satellite increased. Part of the cause of this rise in temperature was that there was no atmosphere to soften the sun's rays. Ride knew that if the satellite overheated, the risk of malfunction increased. Ride determined that it was necessary to turn off the satellite's systems to cool them down. She and her colleagues brainstormed for other possible ways to lower the temperature of the satellite. She reasoned that in the direct sunlight the satellite heated up, but in the shadow of the shuttle, it would cool down. The decision was made to try to move the shuttle so that it would cast a shadow on the satellite, thus hastening the cooling-down process. After a great deal of effort, the commander and pilot moved *Challenger* into the right location. Ride had helped prevent a potentially serious problem.

At one point the satellite's television camera took pictures of the shuttle. This was the first time that the shuttle had ever been photographed in space. The pictures of the shuttle in space, framed against the cloud-covered earth, made *Challenger* look like a "giant extraterrestrial moth."[5] Capcom Guy Gardner at Mission Control voiced the opinion of those on earth watching the broadcast: "Beautiful!" *Challenger* pilot Hauck said, "You've got five very happy people up here." Gardner responded, "There are several thousand happy people down here."[6]

The satellite was allowed to float freely for six hours before Ride brought it back on board and stowed it safely in the cargo hold for future missions. The crew rejoiced at the success of the great arm. Crippen proudly told the world, "We've been told some crews in the past have announced, 'We deliver.' Well, for flight seven, we pick up and deliver."[7]

Mission STS-7 accomplished many firsts. Another

first scheduled for STS-7 was to make the return landing in Florida and not in California. If the shuttle orbiter did not have to be moved from California to Florida, then NASA would save time and money. Thousands of people had already begun to gather at Cape Canaveral. President Reagan also planned to be present for this historical event.

The Florida weather, however, refused to cooperate. At one point Mission Control considered delaying reentry for another day until the weather cleared. The *Challenger* astronauts were delighted with this prospect. When President Reagan heard about the situation, he chose not to go to Cape Canaveral because he did not want his presence to influence the decision of where to land *Challenger*. Lieutenant General James Abrahamson, head of the shuttle program, told the *Challenger* crew to change the reentry time and start their long glide home to the desert runway at Edwards Air Force Base in California.

The crew prepared for reentry. The astronauts put on special pants for their return to earth. A series of tubes in the pants' lining can be inflated to put pressure on the legs. This is needed in the change from microgravity to gravity, as gravity suddenly pulls their body fluids toward the lower body. As their blood rushes down from the brain, the astronauts can inflate the tubes to keep the blood from gathering in their legs. Without enough blood flowing to the brain, an astronaut would get dizzy and black out.

The computers at Mission Control informed Crippen exactly when to begin reentry procedures. Once the decision is made to land, there are no second chances. When *Challenger's* orbit was about two hundred miles above the ground, reentry procedures began. Traveling at a speed of more than seventeen thousand miles per hour, Crippen initiated the descent of *Challenger.* Soon the spacecraft would land on a runway over half a world away.

Crippen turned the shuttle around so that it was traveling tail first. In this way the OMS, or orbital maneuvering system, engines act as brakes and slow the craft down. Small thrusters are fired for two or three minutes. This reduces the shuttle's speed by about two hundred miles per hour. Crippen turned the shuttle around again after the first de-orbit burn. Upon entering the atmosphere, the temperature on the outside of the shuttle reaches 2,700 degrees Fahrenheit. The heat shield of small ceramic tiles keeps the shuttle from burning up. However, an electrified gas that surrounds the spacecraft bursts into fire, blocking all communication with Mission Control in Houston. At the time of Ride's first flight, radio blackout lasted almost twelve minutes. For those on earth, this is a very tense time. There is always the fear that the shuttle will burn up during reentry.

On earth the crowds that had gathered in Florida held their breath during this painfully long blackout period. The NASA pilots who were to follow the shuttle and photograph its reentry searched the skies. The whole mission of each of these planes was to take one infrared picture showing the underside of *Challenger* while it was still very hot. This would give NASA engineers information to further improve the design of the heatshield.

Finally the world heard the cry from the observatory plane: "The tracker has it." Immediately the telescope aboard the special rebuilt transport plane snapped its one picture. From thirty-two miles away, the camera took a picture of the shuttle moving at nearly sixteen times the speed of sound. Lower-altitude chase planes came in for action pictures of the approach and landing. Crippen took over control from the computers and lined *Challenger* up with the black painted stripe on a white patch of desert below him. After six days, two hours, and twenty-four minutes—and ninety-eight orbits around the earth—*Challenger* made a perfect landing.

Five very happy astronauts returned to earth after a successful mission. Challenger *made a perfect landing at Edwards Air Force Base in California on June 23, 1983.*

Much to the disappointment of those who had gathered in Florida, this perfect landing was thousands of miles away in California. There were only a few people on hand to greet the history-making crew as it returned to earth. One handwritten sign read, "Herstory made today by Sally Ride."[8]

The capcom for the mission relayed a message to the crew, "The good news is that the beer is very, very cold this morning. The bad news is that it is three thousand miles away."[9] President Reagan phoned the crew. Talking to Ride, he said, "You were the best person for the job."[10]

Ride's family, of course, had traveled to Florida. After the landing in the California desert, Joyce Ride, disappointed at not being able to greet her older daughter immediately upon her return to earth, said, "We live only a hundred miles from the California runway. We could have stayed home."[11]

Upon returning to the earth, Ride said:

It feels much more difficult physiologically. Your heart rate doubles . . . you turn your head and the whole room spins, your arms and legs feel very heavy, you feel like the book that you were just able to float in front of you now weighs three hundred pounds. . . . The reason that they don't open the hatch early and let the crew out is because the crew literally could not walk down the stairs. You can stand, but you cannot walk in a straight line.[12]

It takes some time for the astronauts to adjust to this one g environment again when they return to the earth.

Mission STS-41-G

The years following Ride's historic flight were filled with public appearances as well as continued training for future flights. Ride had thousands of invitations to speak to various groups around the world. However, she still said that she had done nothing special and that she was not any different from her male colleagues. Whenever an invitation came just because she had been on flight STS-7, she said no. She would go only when the whole crew was included.

In spite of all of her attempts to live a life out of the spotlight, the media would not let Sally Ride off so easily. She was bombarded daily with requests to appear on television or on the radio, or to speak at some gathering. Finally, she recognized that even though she had not chosen to become an astronaut just to become famous, she was in fact famous. She said, "I've come to realize that I will be a role model."[1]

Part of an astronaut's job is to go on speaking tours for NASA. Ride enjoyed this aspect of being an astronaut. She said, "When I go out and give talks at schools and an eight-year-old girl in the audience raises her hand to ask me what she needs to do to become an astronaut, I like that. It's neat! Because now there really is a way. Now it's possible."[2]

Ride has been honored by a wide variety of groups. For example, the seven hundred women employees of NASA honored her as a leader in the field of equal opportunity in the workplace. She and fellow crew members were honored at a state dinner at the White House. Her space suit was given to the Smithsonian National Air and Space Museum in Washington, D.C. She was even invited to give a lesson on the letter *A* for *Sesame Street* by helping Oscar the Grouch prepare for a trip into space. *Ms.* magazine honored her by placing her on the cover of the January 1983 issue. New York City's Mayor Edward Koch presented the whole shuttle crew with keys to the city. In return the crew gave him a collection of photographs of the flight.

The pace of the celebrity was grueling. Yet despite her busy schedule of public events and celebrations, Ride continued in NASA's astronaut training program. There were always new things to learn. On each trip into space, astronauts reported items and procedures that needed to be corrected or improved. Also, each

Sally Ride stands in the mid deck of the orbiting space shuttle. "I've come to realize that I will be a role model," she said after her flight in the Challenger. *As the first American woman in space, she became an inspiration for young girls across the United States.*

mission took new experiments into space. Mission specialist Ride needed to learn about all the changes and the new experiments. Ride discovered that the training was even more helpful the second time around. She knew what a launch felt like, so when she worked in the simulator she could focus her attention on what would help make her next trip easier. She also knew what it was like to live in microgravity for nearly a week. She prepared vigorously for her second flight, which was scheduled for October 1984.

In the meantime, the shuttle program was in full swing. Only two months after the return of STS-7, NASA launched STS-8, which had the distinction of performing the first night launch and landing. It also carried the first African-American astronaut, Guion Bluford, Jr. In November 1983, NASA launched six astronauts in the shuttle *Columbia* STS-9. This mission marked the first flight of Spacelab 1. In February 1984, the *Challenger* STS-41-B crew tried the Manned Maneuvering Unit (MMU) in a space walk for the first time. Previous space walkers had been attached to the main spacecraft with a tether, but with the MMU the astronauts used small jet packs on their backs to travel away from the shuttle. In April 1984 the United States repaired a satellite in orbit for the first time. On August 30, 1984, in the shuttle *Discovery* STS-41-B, Sally Ride's husband, Steven Hawley, had a turn. This flight also carried the first astronaut from private industry, and Judith Resnik, another woman from Ride's training class. Less than two months later, Ride and six other astronauts, the largest crew so far, flew in *Challenger* STS-41-G. This was the first flight with two women on board: Sally Ride and Kathryn Sullivan.

After the rush of publicity about Ride's first flight, media coverage had tapered off considerably. Judith Resnik had been in space in the meantime. Women in space were no longer a great media event. The fact that Kathryn Sullivan was the first American woman to walk in space barely rated a passing nod. What Ride had insisted earlier, that men and women were just doing a job and the fact that women were astronauts should not be considered a big event, was coming true. Women were now part of the NASA space program. NASA's shuttle program was sending shuttles into space so often that the general public was losing interest. The novelty of the space program and of women in space had worn off. People no longer stopped whatever they were doing to watch a launch either from the beach in Florida or on television sets around the world.

The world in general did not seem to care much that on October 5, 1984, NASA launched its one hundredth spaceflight and that two of the astronauts were women. It was also Robert Crippen's fourth flight. The payloads on this flight included OSTA-3, MAPS, and FILE. OSTA, named for NASA's Office of Space and Terrestrial Applications, involved upgraded radar instruments. MAPS included instruments for measuring air pollution from space. FILE was the Feature Identification and Landmark Experiment. On this particular mission the crew also launched a satellite that was important to scientists interested in the earth's weather patterns.

Ride, in her training gear, floats in the ocean after a routine drill. Experience from her first flight helped her train for her second.

Through data collected by this satellite, scientists could determine how much solar energy was reflected back into space by the earth's atmosphere. They were particularly interested in the greenhouse effect, which makes the earth warmer. On this mission, Ride was responsible for launching the weather satellite.

The flight crew for STS-41-G included commander Robert Crippen (the commander of Ride's first flight), pilot John McBride; and five specialists. Ride, Sullivan, and an aeronautical engineer named David Leestma served as mission specialists. Paul Scully-Power, an Australian oceanographer, and Mar Garneau of Canada served as payload specialists. This flight was not as problem free as Ride's earlier flight. One of the first tasks involved launching the weather satellite, primarily Ride's responsibility. She soon discovered that the hinges on the solar panels of the satellite had frozen while it was in the cargo bay. Ride asked Crippen to reposition *Challenger* so that the heat of the sun could shine on the satellite, thus melting the frozen hinges. The sun heated the hinges, everything worked, and the satellite was launched successfully. Once again Ride showed that she could adjust to unexpected problems and come up with quick solutions.

One of the traditions that NASA developed was to wake up the crew with some music after their first night's sleep. Ride and the STS-41-G crew were awakened by the theme song from the movie *Flashdance.* However, the crew had its own plan. They played back a prerecorded message for Houston: "The crew is temporarily out. Please leave your name and address so that we may return your call later on."[3]

The playfulness that was characteristic of Ride's earlier mission had begun.

A surprising coincidence on this mission was the discovery that the two women on this flight, Sally Ride and Kathryn Sullivan, had been in the same second-grade class at the same school. Never did those two little girls in the second grade imagine that thirty years later they would be astronauts together in a space shuttle.

Unfortunately, Ride's second flight was besieged by many small mechanical difficulties. She had to use the robotic arm to fold up a large radar panel that refused to close. Sullivan's walk in space had to be postponed for two days until an air-conditioning problem was fixed. Still, on October 11, 1984, Sullivan and Leetsma walked in space to test the mechanism designed to help with refueling satellites in the future. Overall, the mission was a success in spite of a number of small problems.

Scully-Power, the oceanographer, made some interesting discoveries while on this flight. He was studying special water-current patterns called spiral eddies. From the vantage point of space, he was able to observe the interconnectedness of these spiral eddies throughout the Mediterranean Sea. He also made the first observations of spiral eddies in the Gulf Stream.

The crew landed *Challenger* safely at Kennedy Space Center Shuttle Landing Facility in Florida despite the threat of Hurricane Josephine. Later, problems were identified in the heat shield. Four thousand tiles needed to be replaced before the next mission. This was a serious reminder of the importance of these tiles during shuttle reentry, when the temperature on the outside of the shuttle soars.

Ride's second flight carried the largest-ever United States crew into space. Upon returning, Ride commented, "We bumped into each other a lot, spilled each others' food a lot. We came back and recommended that seven was really the maximum crew size without a space module or bigger living space."[4]

After her second flight, Ride continued to travel on goodwill tours for NASA, speaking to groups around the country. In addition, she received many honors. In June 1985 Anne Morrow Lindbergh presented her with the Lindbergh Eagle Award. The United States Department of Labor minted two gold medallions in her likeness. She received the Jefferson Award from the American Institute of Public Service. In February 1985 she was honored during the Salute to the American Hero event at Disneyland.

In the meantime, NASA's shuttle program marched on toward one of its goals of making space travel available to more people. So far the shuttle expeditions had proved that space travel could indeed be a safe adventure. New projects and experiments were being designed, and NASA had more than one hundred flights scheduled for the next decade. People from all walks of life applied to fly in the shuttle. For civilians, the training was rigorous but not as long. With so many trained astronauts on board, NASA felt that civilians did not need all the same technical expertise. Crews were being created for many future flights. Ride prepared for her third trip into space.

NASA after *Challenger*

On January 28, 1986, the world, the United States, and NASA experienced a terrible tragedy. *Challenger* mission STS-51-L, carrying Richard Scobee, Michael Smith, Ronald McNair, Ellison Onizuka, Judith Resnik, Gregory Jarvis, and civilian Christa McAuliffe, exploded seventy-three seconds after takeoff. All seven people aboard died. Ride, listening to the launch on the radio, refused to believe what her radio was telling her. The astronauts who lost their lives that morning were Ride's colleagues. Launches into space had become so routine that people began to forget about the serious danger involved in each launch and landing. The impact of the explosion slowly began to affect Ride, who said:

I think my first reaction was that I had just lost friends and people I'd gotten a lot of respect for. When I realized how fast it happened, I guess it sort of hit home to me that during a launch that's not what you're thinking about. I don't think they had any indications.[1]

One of the astronauts to lose her life that day was Judith Resnik, one of the six women in the astronaut class of 1978. Ride and Resnik had shared years of training together. Resnik and Ride's husband, Steven Hawley, had flown on the same mission only a year and a half before. Ride and other women astronauts were interviewed by *Ms.* magazine in June 1986 about Judith Resnik. In that interview Ride talked about Resnik and reflected on being an astronaut:

I think everyone in the astronaut program appreciates that there are an awful lot of things that could go wrong, that could cause major damage to the space shuttle. And I think that everyone thought that it was just a matter of time until we had some form of accident. But not necessarily a catastrophe like this.[2]

NASA ordered an immediate investigation of the *Challenger* disaster, which had claimed seven lives and destroyed more than a billion dollars' worth of technology. Robert Crippen, the commander of both of Ride's missions into space, was appointed to lead the investigation. Three aircraft and more than a dozen ships searched six thousand square miles of ocean looking for remains of *Challenger*, the fuel tanks, and the solid rocket boosters. These pieces of debris held clues to the cause of the tragedy.

President Reagan thought that an independent commission should investigate why *Challenger* had blown up. He appointed William Rogers, former secretary of state and a New York lawyer, to head the Presidential Commission on the Space Shuttle Challenger Accident. This became known as the Rogers Commission. Sally Ride was selected as the only active astronaut to serve on the commission. Neil Armstrong, a former astronaut and the first person to walk on the moon, served as vice chair. The members included scientists, educators, and businesspeople. President Reagan hoped that a group of people from such diverse backgrounds would be able to present a less biased report than the NASA committee.

After many hours of studying videotapes, photographs, shuttle debris, and interviews with all the people involved in the launch, the Rogers Commission determined that the safety standards in shuttle launches were imperfect. The report identified a major design problem with the shuttle. For years, the NASA staff had known that the O-rings, seals used in the rocket boosters, could cause a problem. Yet, in their attempt to keep the shuttle program on schedule and to stay ahead of the Soviet Union, they had put this problem aside for future study. The evidence showed that the disaster probably could have been prevented.[3] Ride, who rarely showed extremes of emotion, was very angry. "It's hard to stop from getting mad," she said.[4] Ride had been preparing to fly in her third shuttle mission, but after the *Challenger* disaster and what she had learned from the investigation of the commission on which she served, she declared, "I'm not ready to fly again."[5]

Before the shuttle disaster, Ride had been writing a children's book titled *To Space and Back*, describing what it was like to be in space. It was just about ready to go to press when the *Challenger* exploded. After the accident, Ride changed the dedication page in the book. She dedicated the book to her friends and colleagues on *Challenger* mission STS-51-L and to Dr. Elizabeth Mommaerts, her high school science teacher.

In the introduction to the book, she wrote:

> *On January 28, 1986, this book was almost ready to go to the printer, when the unthinkable happened. The space shuttle* Challenger *exploded one minute after liftoff. After the accident I thought a lot about the book, and whether or not I wanted to change any part of it. I decided that nothing except the dedication and the words I write here should be changed.*[6]

As a result of the Rogers Commission report, President Reagan ordered NASA to change its priorities. The purpose of NASA was no longer to be in the business of launching satellites. Reagan believed that the private sector could do a better job and do it far less expensively.

The shuttle program came to a halt. Changes needed to be made not only in the routine safety of the shuttles themselves, but also in how decisions were made at NASA. The Rogers Commission suggested that astronauts with years of experience in space should be involved in management decisions.

Ride was reassigned to NASA headquarters in Washington, D.C. She became the first working astronaut to cross the line into administration. Her title was special assistant to the administrator for strategic planning. She was assigned to "step back and look at the big picture."[7] New goals for NASA were needed. Thirty years after NASA was established, groups within NASA disagreed with one another about NASA's goals for the end of the century. Some wanted a return to the moon. Others, especially scientists interested in space, wanted to send astronauts to Mars. Ride said:

> *We've been getting a lot of help from outside groups who say that NASA has no vision, no focus. And I think it's fair to say that over the last few years we've definitely lost sight of what our goals are. For example, our goal isn't anymore just to get a vehicle up in space. It's to do something with the vehicle once we get it there that's important. And the same goes for the space station. I mean, who really cares about a building in space? What you care about is what you can do in the building once you're there.*[8]

One of the major documents to be published during this time was a report Ride wrote on leadership at NASA, titled *Leadership and America's Future in Space*. This report sided slightly more with those who wanted a return to the moon. In this sixty-three-page report, Ride analyzed four options for America's future in space. Ride's main goal was to get NASA back on track. She argued for a set of goals that would broaden NASA's purpose. It was not enough to be single-minded

After two successful missions in the space shuttle cockpit, Sally Ride made a change into the management side of NASA. Instead of looking to the sky as an astronaut, she would be looking ahead to the future of the space program.

about getting to Mars before the Russians. Ride said that getting to Mars should not be the goal, but getting to Mars should be part of a larger plan. "It would not be good strategy, good science or good policy," she wrote, "for the U.S. to select a single initiative, then pursue it single-mindedly. . . . Settling Mars should be our eventual goal, but it should not be our next goal."[9] "A commitment to Mars," she warned, "could imperil NASA's plans to put a shuttle fleet back in operation and build a space station. It would also require a tripling of the agency's budget during the mid-90s."[10]

In *Leadership and America's Future in Space*, Ride suggested that NASA focus on four major areas: (1) Mission to Planet Earth: a program that would use the perspective afforded from space to study and characterize our home planet on a global scale. (2) Exploration of the Solar System: a program to retain United States leadership in exploration of the outer solar system, and regain United States leadership in exploration of comets, asteroids, and Mars. (3) Outpost on the Moon: a program that would build on and extend the legacy of the Apollo program. Americans would return to the moon to continue exploration, to establish a permanent scientific outpost, and to begin prospecting the moon's resources. (4) Humans to Mars: a program to send astronauts on a series of round-trips to land on the surface of Mars, leading to the eventual establishment of a permanent base.[11]

Ride wanted NASA as well as Congress and the private sector to simultaneously plan objectives for all four goals. Ride wrote that the program should have two distinct characteristics:

First, it must contain a sound program of scientific research and technology development. . . . Second, the program must incorporate visible and significant accomplishments; the United States will not be perceived as a leader unless it accomplishes feats which demonstrate prowess, inspire national pride, and engender international respect and a worldwide desire to associate with U.S. space activities.[12]

Leadership and America's Future in Space, now commonly referred as the "Ride Report," did not suggest that the four areas replace what NASA was already doing, but that these areas should be added to NASA's program. It also proposed that each of the initiatives be developed independently of the others.

In an interview with Lynn Sherr of *Ms.* magazine, Ride could not state which of the four goals was her priority, for her job was to be an "unbiased observer." She did, however, offer her opinions on why studying the earth was so important:

The planet we live on is much more fragile than we thought it was. Not that it's going to break apart, but it's very sensitive to the changes that take place on its surface and even in the interior . . . it's important to understand the earth's ecosystem on a global scale and how it's changing. . . . [We need to study] the buildup of greenhouse gases in the atmosphere . . . the buildup of methane in the atmosphere. . . . [and the] potential depletion of the ozone layer . . . we need to know more about the effects of El Niño not only on ocean temperature and currents, but also on the global weather pattern. Then there's acid rain. . . . deforestation in the Amazon. . . .[13]

She suggested that it was important to study the earth from space, using special remote sensing platforms. She called for the people of earth to work together and study the earth and its systems, such as the atmosphere and the oceans, and how the oceans and the atmosphere work together.

During this time Ride helped create the Office of Exploration and served as its administrator. She continued to travel widely, touring Europe and addressing the United Nations. She gave talks describing what it was like to be an astronaut, encouraging young girls and women to become scientists or astronauts. She promoted her book and was inducted into the National Women's Hall of Fame.

On Ride's birthday, May 26, 1987, NASA surprised the nation by announcing that Sally Ride, America's first woman in space, was leaving NASA. Ride commented about her departure: "I've always wanted to go back to a university setting. I've spent many happy years at Stanford, as a student and a graduate. I just got the right offer."[14] The year 1987 was an important one in Ride's life. She left NASA, was divorced from Hawley, and returned home to a new phase of her career in physics.

Life After NASA

After leaving NASA, Ride served for two years as a science fellow for the Center for International Security and Arms Control at Stanford University. When she left NASA she said, "I am confident of the future of our nation's space program. . . . It is in the spirit of challenge that I have accepted a position at Stanford University."[1] At Stanford, she helped train scientists in national security and arms control matters. It was an opportunity for scientists to learn how weapons and other inventions they had designed were being used.

In 1989, she left Stanford for San Diego, where she was appointed director of the California Space Institute, University of California, San Diego, in charge of space-related activities. Ride, primarily a physicist, was now free to follow her own research interest, the theory of free electron lasers. Over the years she has published several articles on the topic.

A laser is a very powerful and focused light source. In many sources of light, like the sun or a lightbulb, the light shines in many directions and includes many frequencies (colors) of light. To a physicist, these frequencies of light include the visible colors our eyes can detect and many frequencies our eyes cannot see, such as infrared, ultraviolet, and microwave. The light from a laser is special because it is focused in a very narrow beam. Each type of laser produces one specific frequency of light that may or may not be visible to the eye. Lasers are made to deliver a lot of energy with one frequency of light to a small target area.

It is important to study what happens to laser beams in different environments and situations. Most of Ride's work on lasers contributes to the general knowledge about how lasers work. This research provides data for others, who then find new uses for lasers. For example, lasers are now used extensively in medicine. Laser surgery is fast replacing other forms of surgery. Laser surgery has been shown to reduce risk to the patient and shorten the time a patient is hospitalized. Ride and other physicists doing research on lasers often make the first discoveries on the pathway to these technological advances.

In recent years Ride has become an outspoken advocate for improved science education in public schools in the United States. In spite of her earlier reluctance to claim importance as the first American woman in space, she has recently decided that helping girls and young women gain math and science skills is a priority. It has even become a personal crusade for her.

In addition to her duties as director of the California Space Institute, she was instrumental in developing "KidSat: Mission Operations," an innovative science education program for students of all ages. Ride, along with Dr. JoBea Way, a scientist at the Jet Propulsion Laboratory in Pasadena, California, believed that KidSat would "revolutionize the static curriculum currently implemented in middle schools."[2] In 1995 Ride and Way received $3 million from NASA to develop this three-year pilot project. Three schools were involved in the project: Gompers Middle School in San Diego; Buist Academy in Charleston, South Carolina; and the Washington Accelerated Learning Center in Pasadena, California.

The project directly involved students in the space shuttle program. (The space shuttle program had resumed in 1988 with the flight of *Discovery* STS-26.) The students were required to plan, coordinate, and direct real research aboard the shuttle. When Ride was a mission specialist during her two shuttle flights, she had performed and monitored the getaway specials—those experiments suggested by people outside NASA, some of whom were students. Astronauts on other flights also performed similar tasks, often taking many pictures for analysis by students back on the earth. For the KidSat program, a camera was mounted in the shuttle orbiter's flight

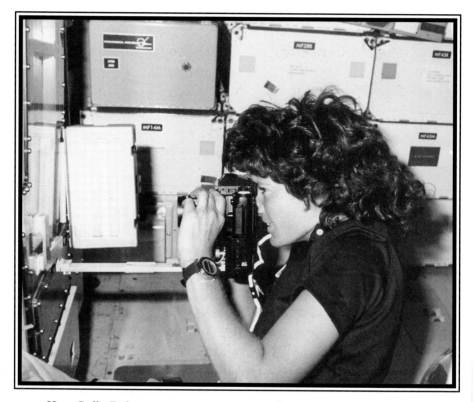

Here Sally Ride uses a camera as part of a science experiment she conducted on board the shuttle. On the ground a few years later, Ride started a school science program in which students could plan real scientific research that would be carried out in space.

deck. This camera was designed to take pictures of the earth and transmit them back to the schools. One of the hallmarks of this new, innovative program designed by Ride and Way was that the students controlled the camera themselves via computer setups in their schools. The students in the classrooms were engaged in real-time data collection.

The data collected by the students was not just random picture taking. Each group of students designed a particular experiment in one of three modules. In the Remote Sensing module, students studied concepts related to earth-viewing instruments in low earth orbit—an orbit between one hundred and a few hundred miles above the earth. In the second module, students studied concepts in orbital mechanics. They were able to use NASA-generated tracking maps to locate sites on photographs. The third module, the Applications-Water module, involved study of water-related features of the earth, such as icebergs and water erosion. Ride and Way wanted students to experience real science in the real world, rather than just learn about science in the classroom.

The students in KidSat were not given special privileges just for being in the program. Each request had to meet NASA's mission operations standards. Each group made an official proposal to NASA through its school's Student Mission Operations Center to the Gateway. The Gateway of the Mission Operations was designed and supervised by students in San Diego's teacher education program.

The Gateway was a mini-version of the new Mission Control Center at the Johnson Space Center in Houston, Texas. The students in the Gateway part of the project are high school students in California's School-to-Career Program. The students at this level of the project receive the image requests from the middle school students. It is their job to assign appropriate orbit segments to each group. The requests are then sent to the computer connected to the camera on the shuttle.

The first test of the KidSat program was in April 1996, with students in middle school, high school, and college. Ride, along with Dr. Michael Wiskerchen, physicist, and Fred Peters, thirty-five-year veteran of NASA, worked with the graduate and undergraduate students in the project. The college students taught the high school students the operation of the Mission Control Gateway. The high school students, along with the college students, oversaw the operations of the Student Mission Operations Centers in the middle schools. Ride and Way would like this new way of teaching science to become a model for science education in the United States.

In keeping with her special interest in helping more young people, both boys and girls, become interested in science, Ride has written three books for children. In *To Space and Back*, she describes what it is like to be an astronaut in space for an extended period of time. In *Voyager: An Adventure to the Edge of the Solar System*, she describes the travels and discoveries of *Voyager I* and *II*, spacecraft that sent data back to earth about the planets in the solar system. *Voyager I* passed Jupiter in 1979 and Saturn in 1980. In 1986 *Voyager II* passed Uranus on its

Ride enjoyed her flight training in the T-38 jet so much that she decided to get her pilot's license. Today, she is happy when she can find time in her busy schedule to fly a Grumman Tiger aircraft.

journey to Neptune, which it passed three and a half years later. In *The Third Planet: Exploring the Earth from Space*, Ride discusses the earth's environment and the impact that human life is having on the planet.

Ride continues to be invited to speak around the world. In addition to her very intensive speaking schedule, she is a member of many committees. In 1996, some of the committees she served on included the National Academy of Sciences Advisory Committee for Television Activities, the President's Committee of Advisors on Science and Technology, and the World Resources Institute Global Council.

She continues to receive many awards and honors. Among them are the J.C. Penney Juanita Dreps Award, the Jefferson Award for Public Service, and the Lawrence Sperry Award, AIAA. She received five NASA Group Achievement Awards, five NASA Special Achievement Awards, and two National Spaceflight Medals. The American Institute of Physics gave her the Science Writing Award.

She continues to enjoy flying. When she can find a few minutes in her extremely busy life, she flies a Grumman Tiger aircraft.

Ride left the California Space Institute as director in 1996. She continues to teach in the physics department at the University of California, San Diego, where she focuses her attention on developing creative and innovative science education strategies for students in America's public schools. Although Ride left NASA in 1987, she continues to inspire all who want to push back the frontiers of space.

1951— Sally Ride is born on May 26 in Los Angeles, California.

1969— Graduates from Westlake School for Girls; attends Swarthmore College, Pennsylvania.

1973— Graduates from Stanford University.

1975— Receives master's degree in physics from Stanford University.

1978— Receives Ph.D. in astrophysics from Stanford University; adjunct professor, space sciences, Rice University; enters NASA training program.

1982— Marries Steven Hawley.

1983— First U.S. woman in space, aboard STS-7.

1984— Second flight aboard STS-41-G.

1985— Assigned to third shuttle flight.

1986— Space shuttle *Challenger* accident; serves on the presidential commission investigating the shuttle accident; assigned to NASA headquarters in Washington, D.C.; publishes *To Space and Back*.

1987— Science fellow, Center for International Security and Arms Control, Stanford University; publishes *Leadership and America's Future in Space*; divorced from Steven Hawley; leaves NASA.

1989— Director, California Space Institute, University of
–1996 California, San Diego.

1989— Professor of physics, University of California,
–present San Diego.

1992— Publishes *Voyager: An Adventure to the Edge of the Solar System*.

1994— Publishes *The Third Planet: Exploring the Earth from Space*.

Chapter Notes

Chapter 1

1. Sally K. Ride, *To Space and Back* (New York: Lothrup, Lee & Shepard, 1986), p. 17.

2. Ibid., p. 18.

3. NASA recording of flight STS-7.

4. Ride, pp. 21–23.

Chapter 2

1. Jerry Adler, "Sally Ride: Ready for Liftoff," *Newsweek*, June 13, 1983, p. 45.

2. Jane Hurwitz and Sue Hurwitz, *Sally Ride: Shooting for the Stars* (New York: Fawcett Columbine, 1989), p. 11.

3. Ibid., p. 13.

4. Adler, p. 49.

5. Ibid.

6. Carolyn Blacknall, *Sally Ride: America's First Woman in Space* (New York: Macmillan, 1984), p. 16.

7. Frederic Golden, "Sally's Joy Ride into the Sky," *Time*, June 13, 1983, p. 57.

Chapter 3

1. Frederic Golden, "Sally's Joy Ride into the Sky," *Time*, June 13, 1983, p. 58.

2. Carolyn Blacknall, *Sally Ride: America's First Woman in Space* (New York: Macmillan, 1984), p. 21.

3. Jerry Adler, "Sally Ride: Ready for Liftoff," *Newsweek*, June 13, 1983, p. 49.

4. Golden, p. 57.

5. Blacknall, p. 20.

6. Adler, p. 45.

7. Ibid., p. 38.

8. Golden, p. 58.

9. Jane Hurwitz and Sue Hurwitz, *Sally Ride: Shooting for the Stars* (New York: Fawcett Columbine, 1989), p. 22.

Chapter 4

1. *Historical Origins of the National Aeronautics and Space Administration* (Washington, D. C.: National Aeronautics and Space Administration, 1962), p. 4.

2. Ibid., p. 5.

3. Ibid., p. 15.

4. Jane Hurwitz and Sue Hurwitz, *Sally Ride: Shooting for the Stars* (New York: Fawcett Columbine, 1989), p. 20.

5. Ibid., p. 33.

6. Ibid., p. 18.

7. Jerry Adler, "Sally Ride: Ready for Liftoff," *Newsweek*, June 13, 1983, p. 49.

8. Hurwitz and Hurwitz, p. 23.

9. Ibid., p. 25.

10. Carolyn Blacknall, *Sally Ride: America's First Woman in Space* (New York: Macmillan, 1984), pp. 42–43.

11. Hurwitz and Hurwitz, p. 25.

12. Blacknall, p. 24.

Chapter 5

1. Carolyn Blacknall, *Sally Ride: America's First Woman in Space* (New York: Macmillan, 1984), pp. 33–34.

2. Ibid., p. 35.

3. Jerry Adler, "Sally Ride: Ready for Liftoff," *Newsweek*, June 13, 1983, p. 49.

Chapter 6

1. Fred Bruning, "A Ticket to a Boring Sally Ride," *Maclean's*, July 25, 1983, p. 9.

2. Ibid.

3. Ibid.

4. Jerry Adler, "Sally Ride: Ready for Liftoff," *Newsweek*, June 13, 1983, p. 36.

5. Mary Virginia Fox, *Women Astronauts Aboard the Shuttle* (New York: Julian Messner, 1984), p. 16.

6. Sally K. Ride, *To Space and Back* (New York: Lothrup, Lee & Shepard, 1986), p. 17.

7. *Microgravity: A Teacher's Guide with Activities for Physical Science* (Washington, D.C.: National Aeronautics and Space Administration, 1995), p. 1.

8. Ride, p. 31.

9. Ibid.

Chapter 7

1. Sharon Bedley, "Challenger's Happy Landing," *Newsweek*, July 4, 1983, p. 70.

2. Mary Virginia Fox, *Women Astronauts Aboard the Shuttle* (New York: Julian Messner, 1984), p. 33.

3. Ibid.

4. Frederic Golden, "Mission Accomplished," *Time*, July 4, 1983, p. 26.

5. Ibid.

6. Ibid.

7. Bedley, p. 70.

8. Ibid., p. 68.

9. Ibid.

10. Golden, p. 26.

11. Bedley, p. 68.

12. Jane Hurwitz and Sue Hurwitz, *Sally Ride: Shooting for the Stars* (New York: Fawcett Columbine, 1989), p. 79.

Chapter 8

1. Jane Hurwitz and Sue Hurwitz, *Sally Ride: Shooting for the Stars* (New York: Fawcett Columbine, 1989), p. 69.

2. Karen O'Connor, *Sally Ride and the New Astronauts: Scientists in Space* (New York: Franklin Watts, 1983), p. 9.

3. Hurwitz and Hurwitz, p. 77.

4. Ibid., p. 80.

Chapter 9

1. Lynn Sherr, "Remembering Judy," *Ms.*, June 1986, p. 57.

2. Ibid.

3. Jane Hurwitz and Sue Hurwitz, *Sally Ride: Shooting for the Stars* (New York: Fawcett Columbine, 1989), p. 84.

4. Ibid.

5. Ibid., pp. 86–87.

6. Sally K. Ride, *To Space and Back* (New York: Lothrup, Lee & Shepard, 1986), p. 9.

7. Lynn Sherr, "A Mission to Planet Earth," *Ms.*, July/August 1987, p. 180.

8. Ibid.

9. Anastasia Toufexis, "Getting NASA Back on Track," *Time*, August 31, 1987, p. 56.

10. Sally K. Ride, *Leadership and America's Future in Space, A Report to the Administrator* (Washington, D.C.: National Aeronautics and Space Administration, 1987), p. 2.

11. Ibid.

12. Sally K. Ride, "Leadership and America's Future in Space," *Astronomy*, January, 1988, p. 9.

13. Sherr, "Mission," pp. 180–181.

14. Hurwitz, p. 97.

Chapter 10

1. Irwin Goodwin, "Sally Ride to Leave NASA Orbit; Exodus at NSF," *Physics Today*, July 1987, p. 45.

2. Christina Baine, *KidSat: Mission Operations*, program papers.

Further Reading

Blacknall, Carolyn. *Sally Ride: America's First Woman in Space*. New York: Macmillan, 1984.

Cole, Michael D. *John Glenn: Astronaut and Senator*. Springfield, N.J.: Enslow, 1993.

Collins, Michael. *Flying to the Moon and Other Strange Places*. New York: Farrar, Straus, & Giroux, 1976.

Fox, Mary Virginia. *Women Astronauts Aboard the Shuttle*. New York: Julian Messner, 1984.

Gallant, Roy A. *National Geographic Picture Atlas of Our Universe*. Prepared by National Geographic Book Service. Ed. Margaret Sedeen, 1st ed. Washington, D.C.: National Geographic Society, 1994.

Hohler, Robert T. *I Touch the Future*. New York: Random House, 1986.

Hurwitz, Jane, and Sue Hurwitz. *Sally Ride: Shooting for the Stars*. New York: Fawcett Columbine, 1989.

Joels, Kerry Mark. *The Space Shuttle Operator's Manual*. New York: Ballantine Books, 1988.

Kramer, Barbara. *Neil Armstrong: The First Man on the Moon*. Enslow Publishers, 1997.

Long, Kim. *The Astronaut Training Book for Kids*. New York: Lodestar Books, 1990.

Neal, Valerie, Cathleen Lewis, and Frank Winter. *Spaceflight*. New York: Macmillan, 1995.

O'Connor, Karen. *Sally Ride and the New Astronauts: Scientists in Space*. New York: Franklin Watts, 1983.

Ride, Sally, and Susan Okie. *To Space and Back*. New York: Lothrup, Lee & Shepard, 1986.

Index